# Workplace Diversity and Inclusion through Virtual Reality

## A Practical Guide

# Table of Contents

# Chapter 1. Introduction

Immerse yourself into the future of inclusion and diversity with our special report, 'Workplace Diversity and Inclusion through Virtual Reality: A Practical Guide.' A lively yet comprehensive landscape, this report teems with innovative strategies, practical case studies, and incisive expert opinions to expand your horizons beyond traditional practices. As our workplaces become increasingly diverse and globalized, this report could be your golden ticket to unlocking a world of opportunities. Dive in to explore how virtual reality can be leveraged to build educational, empathetic, and engaging environments that transcend geographical and cultural barriers, promoting a workplace culture that's inclusive in the truest sense. This report promises not only a rewarding and exciting read but also seeds a transformation that could propel your organization to the front lines of workplace evolution.

# Chapter 2. Understanding Diversity and Inclusion in the Modern Workplace

Workplaces of the 21st century bear little similarity to those of past generations. Globalization, advancements in technology, workers from diverse cultures, varying ages, gender, races, and physical abilities have redefined the boundaries of a 'typical' workplace. Above all, the understanding of diversity and inclusion is no longer a checkbox in a social compliance form – it is a key element guiding an organization's culture, values, and strategies.

## 2.1. Defining Diversity and Inclusion

Diversity refers to the internal and external qualities that make us unique as individuals. It encompasses a broad range of characteristics, including but not limited to age, ethnic origin, physical abilities, gender, nationality, religious beliefs, sexual orientation, race, and socio-economic status.

On the other hand, inclusion is a behavior: the actions, protocols, and environment that make individuals of diverse backgrounds feel welcome, valued, and that they truly belong. While diversity is a mix, inclusion is making the mix work. It is about ensuring that each unique individual has an equal opportunity to contribute their perspectives, ideas, talents and skills, and explore their full potential in a safe, nurturing work environment.

## 2.2. Importance of Diversity and Inclusion

Diversity and inclusion offer a rich mix of ideas, experiences, and perspectives that can enhance creativity, innovation, and problem-solving. When employees feel included in the decision-making processes, they are often more engaged, committed, and satisfied with their jobs.

Moreover, diverse and inclusive workplaces are more likely to attract and retain top talent, reflecting positively on the company's public image and bottom line. A McKinsey research found that companies with more ethnically and racially diverse executives were 33% more likely to have above-average profitability than companies with low diversity.

## 2.3. The Changing Landscape of Workplace Diversity and Inclusion

The concept of diversity and inclusion in the workplace has undergone significant transformations over the years. Initially perceived as a legal and compliance issue, it has evolved into a strategic imperative aligned with business outcomes. This change in perception is largely due to growing awareness of the myriad benefits of a diverse and inclusive workplace offers.

The increase in diversity and inclusion is leading organizations to reevaluate their practices. It emphasizes not just hiring diverse candidates, but also fostering a culture where diverse perspectives are celebrated, and differences are respected.

## 2.4. Role of Technology in Promoting Diversity and Inclusion

Advancement in technology has made the world smaller, offering organizations access to a global talent pool. Through technology, it is feasible to hire people from different cultures, who speak different languages, and live in different time zones. Moreover, technology also makes it possible to offer flexibility in terms of how, when, and where work is done, making it easier for individuals with different needs and lifestyles to participate actively in the workforce.

Significant strides in technology have opened up a world of possibilities for facilitating and promoting diversity and inclusion at work. From AI-powered hiring tools that facilitate bias-free recruitment to virtual reality experiences designed to cultivate empathy towards minority groups, technology is playing a pivotal role in revolutionizing workplace diversity and inclusion.

## 2.5. Virtual Reality: The Future of Workplace Diversity and Inclusion

One emerging technology that holds significant promise in cultivating diversity and inclusion in the workplace is virtual reality (VR). With its immersive nature, VR has the potential to change the way employees understand and interact with each other.

For instance, VR can be used to create empathy training modules that allow employees to experience what it's like to be in their colleagues' shoes. By providing first-hand exposure to different perspectives, these training programs can help break down stereotypes, challenge unconscious biases, and promote understanding and acceptance among employees of various backgrounds. Similarly, virtual collaboration tools can make remote workers feel more included by simulating a co-located environment.

# 2.6. Conclusion

While much progress has been done, there's still a long journey ahead in achieving true diversity and inclusion in the workplace. As organizations continue to evolve and grow, the ability to nurture an inclusive work environment will be crucial for success. As we move forward into the future, understanding and leveraging technologies like virtual reality will be key to fostering empathy, understanding, and genuine diversity and inclusion.

Investing in diversity and inclusion is not just about building a reputation as a socially responsible organization – it makes good business sense. In this age where innovation drives success, fostering a diverse, inclusive workplace can unlock a wealth of creativity, problem-solving ability, and talent.

# Chapter 3. The Virtual Reality Evolution: An Overview

The evolution of virtual reality is an amalgamation of a range of crucial and ambitious technological innovations, continually transforming and adapting itself to the simultaneous proliferation and diversification of everyday digital experiences. The expeditious advancement in technology, coupled with the increasing demand for immersive experiences, has pushed Virtual Reality (VR) into the spotlight and established it as a cornerstone of a new type of business environment – The Virtual Workplace.

## 3.1. The Genesis of Virtual Reality

The seeds of VR were sown in the 1960s with the Sensorama project, a virtual reality theater system that was a precursor to modern VR technologies. Despite this promising start, further growth hampered due to limited technology and high barriers to entry. It wasn't until the 1990s when technology giant Nintendo tested the waters with its unassuming product - the Virtual Boy. Although not a commercial success, it set an important precedent for subsequent development in VR technology.

## 3.2. Clunky Hardware to Sophisticated Devices

Initial iterations of VR technology were riddled with enormous, unwieldy hardware considered impractical for everyday use. Heavy headsets and pricey equipment were the name of the game, seriously constricting the realm of potential users. However, advances in microelectronics and smart computing significantly improved the quality and practicality of VR devices, increasing their potential usability. While the early 2000s saw notable technological giants making higher investments into the VR space, it was the arrival of the Oculus Rift in 2012 that really put VR on the mainstream map.

## 3.3. From a Gaming Fad to a Business Reality

Initially, VR was prized primarily for its gaming applications. The gaming industry took to VR like a moth to a flame, reveling in the immersive experience it offered. However, this was just the beginning. Over time, as the novelty of the gaming applications began to fade, the potential usability of VR in other industry sectors became increasingly apparent. VR found applications in healthcare, architecture, education, and, notably, business workplace environments.

## 3.4. The Virtual Workplace: A New Frontier

The landscape of work is changing rapidly. With globalization and digitalization reshaping organizations, there's a growing pressure on businesses to adapt. This is where Virtual Reality steps in, heralding a new era of remote working and fostering unprecedented levels of diversity and inclusion in the workplace. Through VR, companies can provide realistic and interactive workplace environments where employees can interact and collaborate regardless of their geographical location. With life-like avatars and real-time interactions, VR challenges traditional definitions of 'workplace'.

## 3.5. The Importance of Software Development

While hardware tends to garner the lion's share of attention when discussing VR, the evolution of VR software has also played an essential role in shaping the technology as we know it today. Sophisticated software is key to creating immersive and engaging virtual environments. Consequently, as the industry continues to progress, the demand for innovative VR software development will undoubtedly surge.

## 3.6. The Future of Virtual Reality

While it's clear that VR has come a long way since its inception, the road to its ultimate destination seems equally exciting. As VR technology continues to evolve, we could see the creation of incredibly immersive and interactive virtual worlds. Further, wireless headsets would make it more accessible to the mainstream audience. Businesses have only scratched the surface of what's possible with VR. For diversity and inclusion efforts, VR holds the potential to bridge gaps, overcome language barriers, and foster a truly global workspace.

In conclusion, the evolution of Virtual Reality paints a storied tapestry of technological innovation, one that continues to challenge our assumptions about the world and our place in it. As VR inches closer and closer to achieving true immersion, it's inclusion in business processes is a guarantee. The only question that remains is just how innovative and transformative these applications will be. Only time can paint this picture with accuracy.

# Chapter 4. Bridging the Gap: Virtual Reality and Its Role in Advancing Inclusion

Diversity and inclusion have been key themes in the workplace discourse over the past decade. Amidst this, a technological marvel, Virtual Reality, has emerged as a vital tool for embracing, promoting, and nurturing D&I. Virtual Reality (VR) extrapolates and simplifies complex real-world scenarios, renders immersive three-dimensional experiences, and importantly, it transcends geographical and socio-cultural boundaries.

## 4.1. Achieving Universal Inclusion with VR

VR, at its core, is an empathy machine, replicating experiences and environment in the most authentic and immersive manner possible. At the intersection of VR and D&I, we find a critical solution to the age-old problem of inclusion. By providing experiences that build understanding and empathy, VR helps unravel cultural nuances and differences without the pressure and constraints attributed to real-life interaction. Put simply, VR creates a safe space for global teams to learn, interact, and collaborate.

For example, virtual onboarding programs can introduce new hires to unique work cultures and expectations, and build a sense of connection and belonging right at the start. They can also simulate different roles, helping employees understand various perspectives within the organization. This immersion can spur a greater appreciation of diverse roles, promoting a culture of mutual respect and collaboration.

# 4.2. VR in Action: Practical Case Studies

1. Breaking Preconceptions with VR Training

Vodafone, a global telecom giant, piloted a VR-based diversity and inclusion training program in 2018. A scenario simulation trained employees on implicit gender biases. This program reported significant increases in employee engagement and decreases in gender bias, corroborating the efficacy of VR.

1. Persona Simulation for Empathy Development

Medical company Novartis launched a VR program creating experiences from the perspective of visually impaired individuals. This helped in developing empathy and understanding towards such persons, leading to improved accommodation and greater workplace inclusivity.

# 4.3. The Power of VR: Bridging the Physical and the Empathetic Gap

Challenges often arise when teams exist across disparate geographies and cultures. Notably, VR provides the perfect solution. Participation in a virtual environment cultivates the familiarity and understanding needed to bridge these gaps. VR sparks cultural exchange and conversation, thereby breaking down any fear or apprehension.

Moreover, VR can help bring isolated or homebound employees into the office environment, fostering a sense of belonging and inclusion. This is particularly invaluable in the current climate where remote working often leaves employees feeling detached and disconnected.

## 4.4. The Future is Here: Embracing VR for Workplace D&I

The potential VR harbors for advancing inclusion is immense. We already have examples of companies demonstrating the benefits of VR-enabled diversity programs: improved team collaboration, reduced biases, and overall more inclusive environments.

However, there are still challenges to overcome, notably the cost and availability of VR gear. As these barriers lower and VR technology becomes more accessible, we can anticipate more widespread adoption, creating a more empathetic, connected, and inclusive world of work.

Through this chapter, we have seen how VR, besides being a technology marvel, is a matchless tool in the hands of D&I practitioners. Its immersive, engaging, and neutral nature has eased the path to universal inclusion, promoting understanding, empathy, and respect in the workplace.

As we move forward, integrating VR into our regular training and culture-building initiatives will not be a mere option, but an inevitable strategy to advance inclusion, empathy, and mutual respect in our diverse, global workplace landscapes.

# Chapter 5. Promoting Empathy and Understanding through Virtual Experiences

A key aspect of fostering an inclusive and diverse working environment involves promoting empathy and understanding among employees. Through true empathy, individuals can better comprehend and connect with the experiences of their colleagues, irrespective of the differences in their backgrounds or perspectives. Today, thanks to advancements in technology, we have a powerful tool right at our fingertips that helps accomplish this: Virtual Reality (VR). Submerging users in a replicated world or a completely imaginary environment, VR can create intensely visceral and immersive experiences that may significantly contribute to building understanding and empathy in the workplace.

## 5.1. The Power of VR in Empathy Building

Let's take a step back and consider traditional methods of fostering empathy and understanding. These often rely on conversations, storytelling, or team-building exercises. Although these methods certainly have their merits, they often fall short when trying to bridge significant cultural, experiential, or psychological gaps. Put simply, it's challenging to truly empathize with a person or understand their experiences solely through spoken or written words without a strong 'visualization' element.

Here is where Virtual Reality steps in. VR transcends the boundaries of conventional empathy-building methods by providing a platform where people can actually 'walk a mile in another person's shoes'. This technology facilitates a cognitive shift that can lead to profound emotional understanding, essentially constituting 'amplified empathy'.

## 5.2. Case Study: Amnesty International's VR Campaign

In 2016, Amnesty International launched a VR campaign that let people rapidly comprehend the gravity of the Syrian crisis. Users were virtually transported to the bombed streets of Syria, highlighting the horrific reality of war in a way that traditional news coverage could never do. The result was a 16% increase in direct-debit donations to the organization, indicating that immersive experience positively influenced individuals' empathy.

## 5.3. Implementing VR for Empathy-Building in Your Organization: Step-by-Step

The implementation of VR as a tool for empathy-building in your organization will require careful planning and thoughtful execution. This section will lay out a detailed roadmap to help your organization adopt VR for this purpose.

1. Define the Objectives: Identify the particular areas or issues where you believe fostering empathy will improve your workplace environment. It could be anything from increasing cultural understanding to sensitizing employees about physical disabilities.

2. Identify the Right VR Tools: Depending on your organization's needs and budget, there are a multitude of VR platforms that you can choose from. This could range from high-end equipment like Oculus Rift to mobile-based systems like Google Cardboard.

3. Create VR Content: This step might involve resource-intensive processes like 3D modeling or simpler alternatives like 360-degree videos. Content should be aimed squarely at achieving your defined objectives.

4. Test and Iterate: Implement the VR experience with a small group first to gather feedback. Enhancement should be a continuous process based on such feedback.

5. Employee Training: Conduct sessions to familiarize employees with the VR equipment and the process.

6. Measurement: Monitor the impact of VR experiences on employee behavior, attitude, and understanding to gauge the effectiveness of the initiative.

## 5.4. Addressing Potential Issues

While the case for VR seems promising, it's important to anticipate possible hurdles when introducing a new and immersive technology. These could include technical difficulties, costs, resistance from employees, or VR induced motion sickness. A phased introduction of VR, coupled with strong organizational communication about its benefits, can help mitigate potential resistance.

## 5.5. The Future of VR and Empathy-Building

The intersection of VR and empathy-building is expected to continue growing and evolving. Experiences are becoming more immersive with advancements like haptic feedback, allowing users to feel virtual items and experiences. Such developments could lead to more effective empathy and understanding in all areas of inclusion and diversity.

In conclusion, incorporating VR into your diversity and inclusion strategies can unlock whole dimensions of empathy and understanding. It provides an avenue for employees to experience, comprehend, and connect with what their colleagues might be experiencing on a day-to-day basis. The practical informational guide above hopes to serve you in implementing such a transformative process in your organization. Through it, you may be able to not just visualize, but actualize an inclusive and diverse workplace reality.

# Chapter 6. Breaking Cultural and Geographical Barriers with Virtual Reality

As we delve into the revolutionary capacity of Virtual Reality (VR) to dismantle cultural and geographical barriers, it's essential to first comprehend the unique blend of technological innovation and intercultural communication that VR presents. Through the lens of VR, we have the power to construct immersive experiences that open the gates to diverse perspectives and understandings.

## 6.1. The Spectrum of VR in Tackling Cultural Barriers

Technological development has always marked its influence on cross-cultural interactions, and VR is at the forefront of such transformative movements. VR transcends conventional modes of communication by fostering rich, lifelike interactions - an almost physical presence in non-physical environments.

Understanding and appreciating different cultures demands more than theoretical knowledge; it requires experiential exposure. This is where VR's potential comes to the fore.

VR can simulate cultural experiences: people can immerse themselves in virtual journeys exploring authentic customs, celebrating local festivals, or appreciating traditional art and music. Experiencing a foreign culture virtually can reduce the risk of miscommunication and cultural conflicts at work.

## 6.2. Virtual Field Trips

Imagine being able to experience a day in the life of a farmer in rural Africa or a chef in Italy. Virtual field trips enable these real-world experiences, and more, that employees might not have the opportunity to experience otherwise. They offer in-depth insights into different lifestyles, economic conditions, and customs that enhance comprehension and empathy, building stronger relationships across teams.

## 6.3. Virtual Reality as a Training Tool

Just as VR serves as a bridge to culturally inclusive education in schools, similar strategies can be implemented in work environments. VR-based training sessions, featuring culturally variable scenarios, offer employees a firsthand cultural experience.

Participants can learn appropriate responses to different situations, improving their cultural sensitivity. For instance, a virtual trip to a business meeting in Japan can expose an employee to their unique business etiquette. Such exposure can form a robust foundation for intercultural communications in a diverse workforce.

## 6.4. Eliminating Geographical Hurdles with VR

In a globalized workplace, companies often face the challenge of conducting conferences and meetings with teams dispersed all over the world. Here lies another avenue where VR has proven to be a game-changer.

Through VR conference rooms, global teams can interact seamlessly as if they were physically present together, breaking down geographical barriers. It's not merely about talking figures or tasks, but it also allows room for interpersonal connections, akin to physical interactions, which are invaluable in building a cooperative work culture.

## 6.5. Virtual Replicas of Real Offices

Creating virtual replicas of real offices is another exciting application of VR. Employees from various parts of the world can put on their VR headsets and find themselves in their company's office, irrespective of their physical location. This can significantly improve a sense of belonging among remote workers and provide a unified office experience.

## 6.6. The Future Perspective

VR technology is still evolving, indicating a promising future where workplaces dominated by homogenic ideologies could become a thing of the past. Innovations are pushing the boundaries of how organizations can harness the power of VR to foster diversity and inclusion.

As we anticipate the emergence of better and more immersive VR technology, a valuable lesson is that this tool's essence remains the same - bridging gaps, breaking down barriers, and enhancing our understanding and appreciation of each other.

Though transforming traditional workplace habits and norms might feel demanding, especially when we're introducing cutting-edge technologies like VR, these transformative steps lead towards a future of workplace diversity and inclusion, unrestricted by geographical or cultural barriers. As we continually navigate through these exciting horizons, one thing is certain: VR is truly revolutionizing the way we perceive, understand, and interact with the world around us.

# Chapter 7. Case Studies: Success Stories of VR in Promoting Workplace Diversity

When it comes to leveraging new technologies for workplace diversity and inclusion, several organizations have taken the lead with Virtual Reality (VR). In the following sections, we analyze some of these scenarios - chalked out as inspiring case studies - offering a glimpse into the power of VR in promoting workplace diversity.

## 7.1. Embracing Different Perspectives with VR: EY's Bold Approach

EY, the multinational professional services firm, invested in VR to instill a deep and shared understanding of the challenges faced by employees with disabilities. Given their diverse and global workforce, EY faced difficulty getting their global staff invested in understanding the perspective of differently-abled individuals.

The VR experience 'Diverse Voices,' developed in collaboration with VR vendors, immersed participants in four different scenarios. Each scenario portrayed the difficulties faced by employees with autism, dyslexia, hearing impairment, and wheelchair users, forcing the participants to literally step into their co-workers' shoes.

Feedback was outstanding; employees emerged with a much more profound understanding of their colleagues' struggles. EY now uses 'Diverse Voices' as a keystone of their corporate diversity and inclusion strategy worldwide.

## 7.2. Breaking Geographic Barriers: The Volvo Virtual Reality Case

Swedish automotive manufacturer Volvo sought to surmount the geographic barrier among its internationally based teams. They partnered with technology companies and adopted VR for their communications needs.

Virtual meetings using impressive immersive 360° experiences with lifelike avatars facilitated rich, seamless interaction between teams located worldwide. This novel approach reduced travel time and costs, led to quicker decision-making, and improved team cohesion. Furthermore, cross-cultural understanding was enhanced as employees could virtually 'visit' facilities across the world, fostering a sense of inclusivity.

## 7.3. Transforming Empathy into Action: Walmart's Training Revolution

Walmart, leading the retail sector, wasn't far behind in leveraging VR technology to foster empathy among its employees towards its varied customer base. They wanted their employees to fully understand and empathize with the customers they serve daily, many of whom come from diverse backgrounds.

Partnering with STRIVR, Walmart developed unique VR scenarios, such as being a single parent on a tight budget or an older person having mobility constraints. The immersive experiences helped employees view situations from their customers' perspectives.

Post-VR training, Walmart noticed an increase in empathetic behaviors towards customers, improved customer service, and more favorable customer feedback.

## 7.4. Enhancing Cultural Competency: The Scenario in the Healthcare Sector

Healthcare workers often interact with patients from diverse backgrounds, making cultural competency training vital. A leading hospital in Boston partnered with a VR company to develop a module aimed at fostering cultural competence.

Staff was involved in virtual scenarios where they interacted with avatars representing patients from varied cultural backgrounds. The reactions of the avatars depended on the cultural sensitivity displayed, thus facilitating experiential learning.

Post-training, the staff reported higher levels of confidence in dealing with patients from diverse backgrounds, leading to improved patient satisfaction levels.

In conclusion, these case studies offer proof that VR holds vast potential in transforming workplaces into diverse and inclusive spaces. Organizations that use this technology effectively not only foster a more empathetic, understanding, and competent workforce, but they also place themselves on the forefront of the digital revolution, proving the potential of VR as a tool for enhancing workplace diversity and inclusion.

# Chapter 8. Practical Implementation: Setting up VR in Your Organization

Practical implementation of Virtual Reality (VR) in the workplace presents a unique set of challenges and opportunities. It's critical to consider all aspects, including budget, employee experience, and organizational culture, among others.

## 8.1. Hardware and Software Solutions

To begin with, hardware and software are the primary building blocks of a VR system. Headsets, controllers, tracking systems, and related materials form the hardware component, which facilitates the immersive experience of VR. These pieces of equipment can vary from standalone units to tethered setups, and it's crucial to choose based on the specific needs and budget of your organization.

On the software side, there are two primary types of application: those that are pre-built solutions available on the market, and those that will be custom-designed and developed according to the specific needs of your organization. Both have their merits, depending on budget, timeline, and use case.

## 8.2. Implementation Strategy

A clear implementation strategy is crucial for the successful incorporation of VR in your organization. Start by defining objectives and measurable outcomes, considering both the scope and scale of the implementation. Consider factors such as who will use the VR equipment and for what purpose, the space and infrastructure required, and how it will mesh with the company's existing tech ecosystem.

Parallelly, assess any potential risks and pitfalls. Understanding challenges in terms of initial costs, maintenance expenses, ongoing technology updates, time commitment for setup and training, are all vital aspects to consider. Also, it's essential to consider potential user discomfort or resistance to adopting VR and address them proactively.

## 8.3. Training and Support

To exploit VR's vast potential, user training is essential. Employees should be prepared to use VR environments smoothly and efficiently, but also be able to troubleshoot minor issues without external assistance. To this end, set up a robust training system that covers everything from the basics of VR to advanced skills as per your organizational needs.

Additionally, provide technical support to address issues that users cannot resolve independently. This team should be equipped to tackle technical hiccups and deliver a seamless VR experience to users.

## 8.4. Inclusion and Diversity Paradigm

How do we ensure the VR experience is inclusivity-oriented? This question should remain central to all processes and strategies. Ensure your content is devoid of potential triggers that could inadvertently cause discomfort to some users, be it due to their cultural, nationality, or physical conditions. Remember, the goal is to promote empathy and understanding, and this should permeate every element of the VR setup.

# 8.5. Management and Reassessment

Lastly, effective management of your VR system includes routine checks, maintenance, and reassessments. Evaluate the success metrics regularly, seek user feedback, and make adjustments as necessary. Remember that technology and business needs evolve with time, so your VR setup should never be static.

Remember, there's no one-size-fits-all approach to setting up VR in an organization. Every company's requirements and constraints are unique. But thorough planning, employee training, inclusion-oriented strategies, proper management, and regular reassessments will help you create an impactful virtual-reality training program that is inclusive, engaging, and effective.

# Chapter 9. Measuring the Impact of Virtual Reality on Inclusion

It's no longer enough to deploy virtual reality (VR) systems and hope for the best. These systems must be monitored and their impact measured, especially in terms of increasing inclusion and diversity in the workplace. In this chapter, we'll delve into some of the effective ways to measure the impact of VR on inclusion.

## 9.1. The Imperative of Impact Assessment

Impact assessment is essential because it shows whether VR measures are making a difference and how they can be improved. Evaluation of these interventions is not always straightforward, particularly when it comes to subjective concepts like diversity and inclusion. However, some tools can serve as indicators of progress: employee surveys, data analysis, and formal/informal feedback, among others.

## 9.2. Well-being Measure

Through VR experiences, we can provide a controlled setting wherein people can learn and adapt to diverse situations without feeling threatened or overwhelmed. Using measures such as decrease in stress levels, increased engagement and satisfaction, and overall mental well-being in the participant's survey can determine how virtual reality impacts inclusivity and diversity from a personal standpoint.

## 9.3. Quantitative Approach: Leverage Your Data

Look at the change in representation from underrepresented groups. Is there an increase in their numbers in different departments or leadership roles as a result of the VR training? Developing a dashboard that centralizes all diversity metrics can simplify the process. It might include recruitment statistics, promotion rates, attrition rates, and more to provide a comprehensive picture of the organization's state of diversity.

## 9.4. Qualitative Approach: Employee Surveys and Interviews

Deeply understanding employee experiences will always require speaking directly to them. Regularly collecting data through surveys and interviews can provide valuable insights into the effectiveness of VR-based diversity training. Inclusion is about embracing differences, so asking people how they perceive diversity and inclusion at different points in their employee experience can guide real-time monitoring and changes.

## 9.5. Training Effectiveness and Skill Acquisition

Is there demonstrable improvement in the understanding of unconscious bias among the employees following the VR training? To measure this, organizations can lean on Kirkpatrick's Four-Level Training Evaluation Model. Start with the participants' reaction (did they feel the training was relevant?), learning retention (were they able to understand the concepts?), behaviour change (are they applying the learning in their job?), and results (by direct observation or 360 feedback).

## 9.6. Feedback from Diversity and Inclusion Leaders

In conjunction with quantitative measurement, organizations could also beneficially leverage the expert opinions of Diversity and Inclusion leaders. These leaders can give feedback, innovative ideas, and constructive criticism to improve the overall approach.

## 9.7. Peer Observations

Enlisting other staff members to observe their colleagues and gather data can be a highly useful strategy. Observations about interactions in group settings can reveal subtler behaviors – such as whether all voices are being heard, or whether unconscious bias is becoming less apparent – that aren't detectable through other means.

VR has been a game-changer in promoting Diversity and Inclusion in the workplace. However, the usefulness of any new tool should be periodically evaluated, and impact measured to ensure it's serving its intended purpose.

In measuring the impacts of VR on Diversity and Inclusion, takeaways can be used to further enhance VR programs, helping organizations arise as leaders in the fight for inclusion, all the while ensuring superior employee engagement and satisfaction. It's an ongoing journey that continues to evolve with technology, people, and societal norms. Technology alone cannot ensure diversity and inclusivity, but it's a powerful tool in the right hands, with the right strategy.

In conclusion, VR's potential to transform workplace training towards a more inclusive future is immense, and with careful and thoughtful evaluation, its impact can be maximized. By measuring its contribution to the broader inclusion objectives, we can continue to refine and improve our approaches, ensuring that every initiative is effective, and every endeavor is resourceful.

# Chapter 10. Future Trends: The Outlook for VR in Workplace Diversity

In looking forward, it's clear that virtual reality (VR) is poised to significantly influence workplace diversity and inclusion. This powerful technology has the potential to change our approach in creating more understanding and empathetic global workplaces. Using VR, we can effectively bridge cultural gaps, challenge biases and unconscious prejudices, all while encouraging increased collaboration amongst diverse teams.

## 10.1. Understanding the Future Power of VR

To comprehend the role VR might play in improving diversity and inclusion, we must first understand the unique features that this technology brings to the table. VR can create immersive, realistic 3D environments that users interact with in real time. With its ability to mimic real-world situations, VR increases the potential for experiential learning. These realistic simulations can be particularly effective in unconscious bias training, allowing employees to literally 'walk in someone else's shoes,' and understand their perceptions, challenges, and experiences.

## 10.2. Challenging Unconscious Bias

According to the World Economic Forum, unconscious bias is one of the biggest obstacles to creating inclusive workplaces. VR has the potential for disrupting this status quo by providing perspective-taking experiences. These simulations help in 'rewiring' the brain, influencing behavior change and attitudes at a fundamental level.

## 10.3. Bridging Cultural Gaps

Workforce globalization necessitates understanding and appreciating cultural differences. VR simulations can provide employees with virtual 'field trips' to different countries, allowing them to experience and understand global cultures' nuances. As a result, VR can foster a more inclusive environment by breaking down cultural barriers and promoting a better understanding of cultural diversity.

## 10.4. Promoting Collaboration and Leading for Inclusion

VR is also making waves when it comes to team collaboration. Through shared VR experiences, geographically dispersed teams can feel a strong connection with each other regardless of their physical location. It's a way to put everybody in the same room, creating an environment for fostering collaboration and connection among diverse teams, which aids in creating an inclusive environment.

In addition to promoting collaboration, VR can also serve as an effective tool for inclusion leadership training. By creating an immersive experience, VR can help leaders better understand the exclusion followers might feel, fostering a more inclusive leadership style.

## 10.5. Accessibility and Accommodation

Diversity also includes physical and mental abilities that often require unique accommodations. VR can create a safe and controlled environment for differently-abled people, providing opportunities to participate fully in the workplace. It can simulate various scenarios and environments, helping organizations to plan and execute accessibility accommodations.

# 10.6. Future Predictions

Looking ahead, VR holds a promising future in enhancing workplace diversity and inclusion. As more organizations adopt this technology, we will likely witness a greater emphasis on creating VR experiences designed explicitly for diversity and inclusion training. We also anticipate the rise of new VR technologies focusing on accessibility, adaptive interfaces, and associated solutions.

Finally, as VR becomes more mainstream, it's essential for organizations to stay informed about the innovative ways VR can enhance workplace diversity and inclusion. The adoption of VR in the workplace is not simply about using the latest tech, but represents a unique opportunity to drive significant culture change towards a more inclusive and diverse work environment.

This chapter only scratches the surface of what VR can do to foster workplace diversity and inclusion. As VR technology continues to evolve, so will the possible applications for diversity and inclusion. There's no doubt that VR will continue to play a groundbreaking role in shaping more inclusive and diverse workplaces in the future.

# Chapter 11. Building a Comprehensive VR Strategy for Diversity and Inclusion

Understanding that diversity and inclusion (D&I) remain integral to a thriving and effective workplace is one thing. Actualizing this understanding with a comprehensive strategy that encompasses all aspects of your organization is an entirely different challenge. As technology evolves, Virtual Reality (VR) presents an exciting solution that can revolutionize the way we approach D&I.

## 11.1. The Rationale for VR in D&I Training

A well-rounded VR diversity training should have concrete reasons for its incorporation. The rationale should hinge on clear-cut benefits and the unique value proposition that VR has over traditional diversity training methods.

VR's immersive nature makes it an excellent tool in imparting empathy, opening people's minds to different perspectives, and aiding in the internalization of the true value of individual distinctions. Participants can directly 'experience' different situations that people from diverse backgrounds go through, which is impossible through conventional training. VR allows for these experiences to be created and shared, sparking awareness and empathy that forms the bedrock of a truly inclusive workplace.

## 11.2. Identifying Key Goals and Objectives

Just like any other strategic initiative, your VR diversity and inclusion strategy must be goal-driven. The first step involves identifying what you hope to accomplish. Determine what the current state of diversity and inclusion in your organization is, and envision the desired future state. Your goals might encompass increasing empathy across teams, reducing unconscious bias, or fostering an inclusive workplace culture.

Also, ensure your goals are SMART: Specific, Measurable, Achievable, Relevant, and Time-bound. This enables you to track progress and evaluate the success of the strategy once implemented.

## 11.3. Stakeholders' Engagement

Securing buy-in from all stakeholders is crucial. The management team must fully support the VR D&I strategy. Also, get HR, line managers, and employees on board. Their participation will ensure a comprehensive understanding of the unique needs and challenges across all levels of the organization.

## 11.4. Choosing the Right VR Training Program

When settling for a VR training platform, consider the diversity and inclusion goals you have set, your budget, and the specific needs of your organization. Whether you're opting for an off-the-shelf VR training solution or a bespoke package, it's crucial to ensure that it fits within the established parameters.

# 11.5. Assembling a Team

Putting a team in charge of the VR D&I strategy is key. The team should comprise members experienced in VR, D&I practices, and change management. They would oversee the rollout of the strategy - from planning, sensitization workshops, to program implementation and progress tracking.

# 11.6. Implementation

Roll out your VR D&I program in stages, testing it with a group first, then scaling to the rest of the organization based on the feedback received. Subsequent improvements may include adjusting VR experiences for more relevance or simplifying interfaces for easier use. Constant process evaluation and feedback are integral at this stage.

# 11.7. Monitoring and Evaluation

Once the VR D&I strategy is fully implemented, its effectiveness should be monitored and evaluated against the set goals regularly. This could involve carrying out surveys or employee interviews to gauge their experience, attitudes, and feelings after the training. Feedback gathered should inform future tweaks and improvements.

# 11.8. Continuous Improvement

Continuous improvement is an essential part of an effective comprehensive VR D&I strategy. After accomplishing some of your smaller targets, it's time to redefine your goals. Aim higher, think bigger, and continue finding ways to infuse more diversity and inclusivity into your company's DNA. Remember, VR D&I isn't a short-term plan. It evolves as your organization evolves.

Tackling diversity and inclusion through VR increases the potential for not just understanding and acceptance, but for personal and professional growth that propels your organization into the future.

www.ingramcontent.com/pod-product-compliance
Lightning Source LLC
Chambersburg PA
CBHW060902260726
48661CB00008B/3400